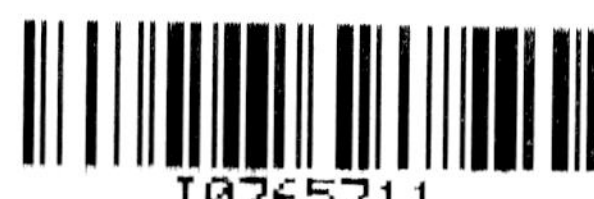

I0765711

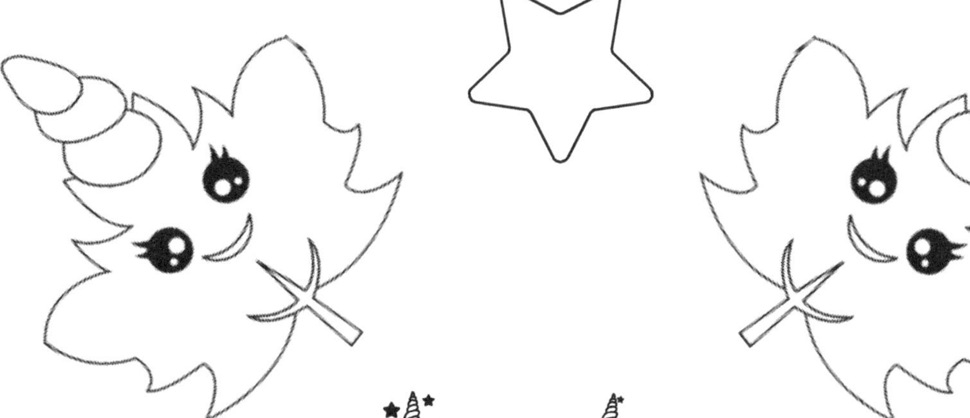

THIS BOOK
BELONGS TO:

____

____

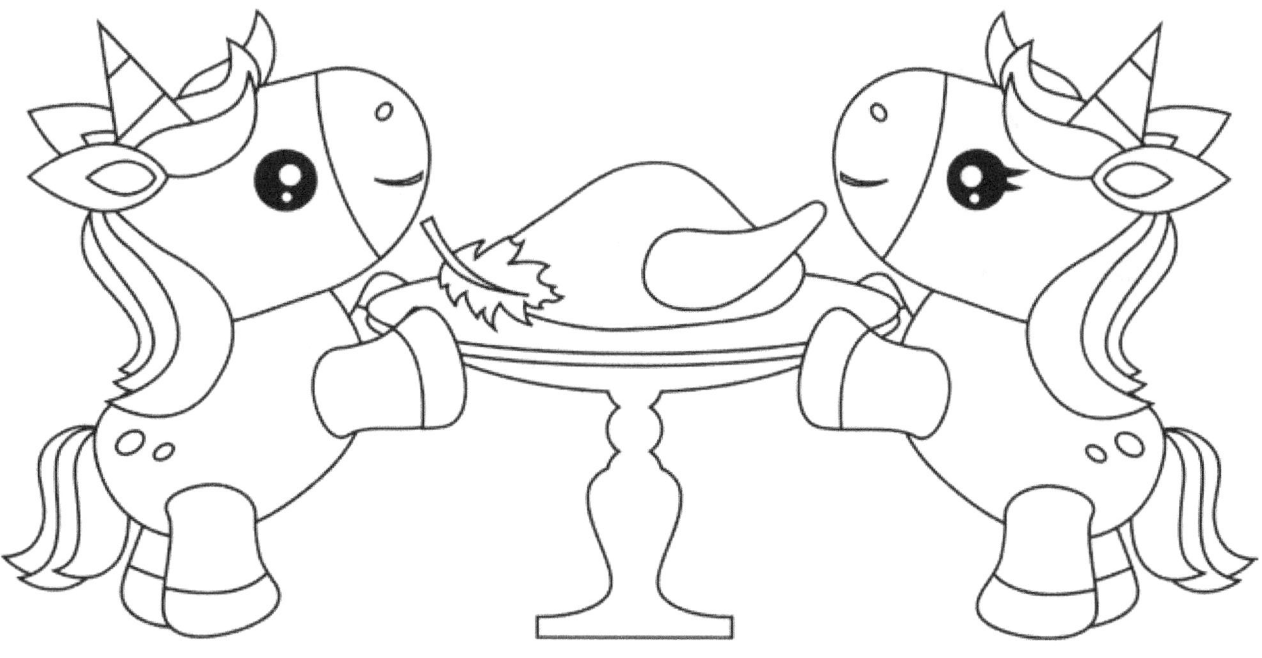

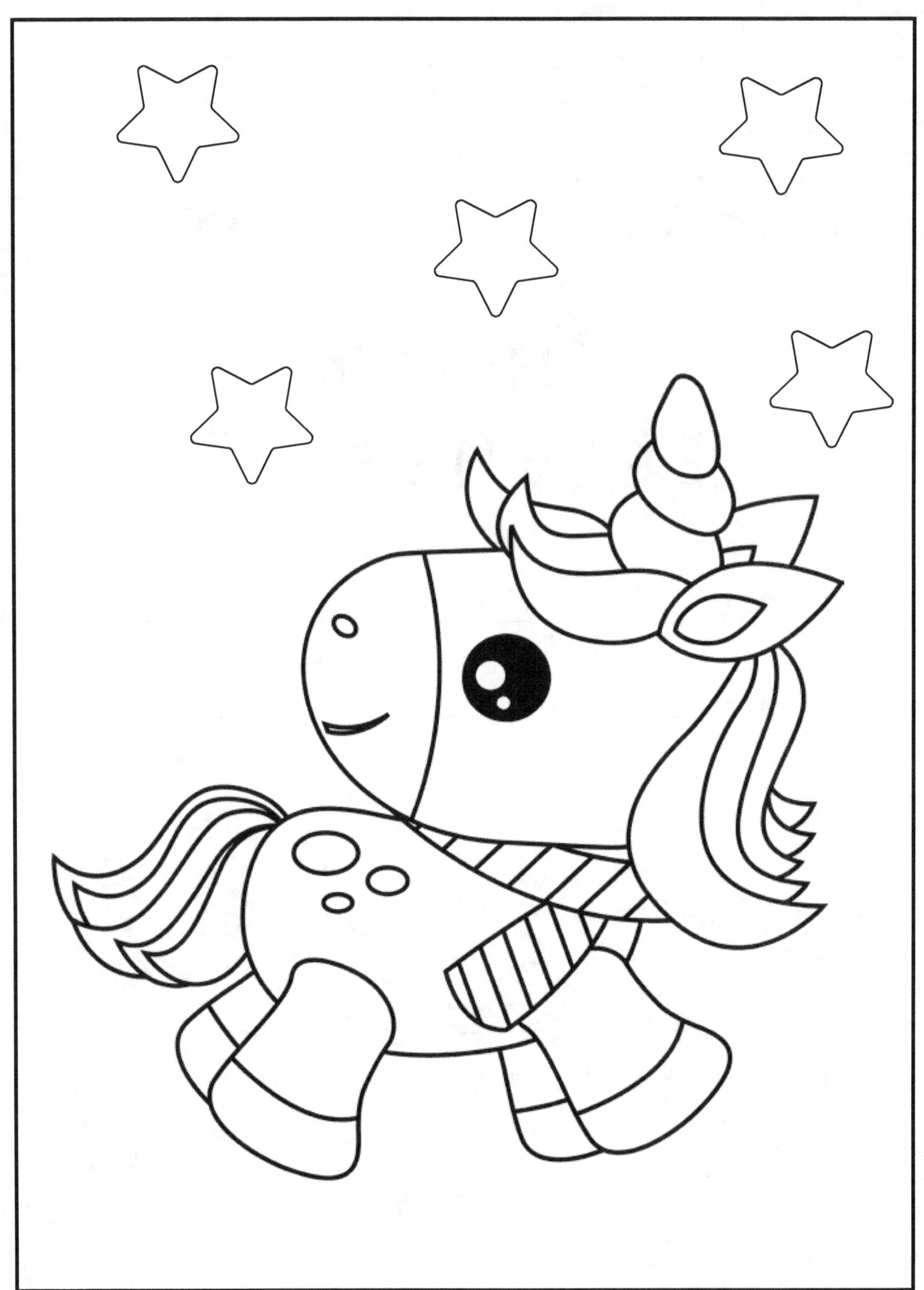

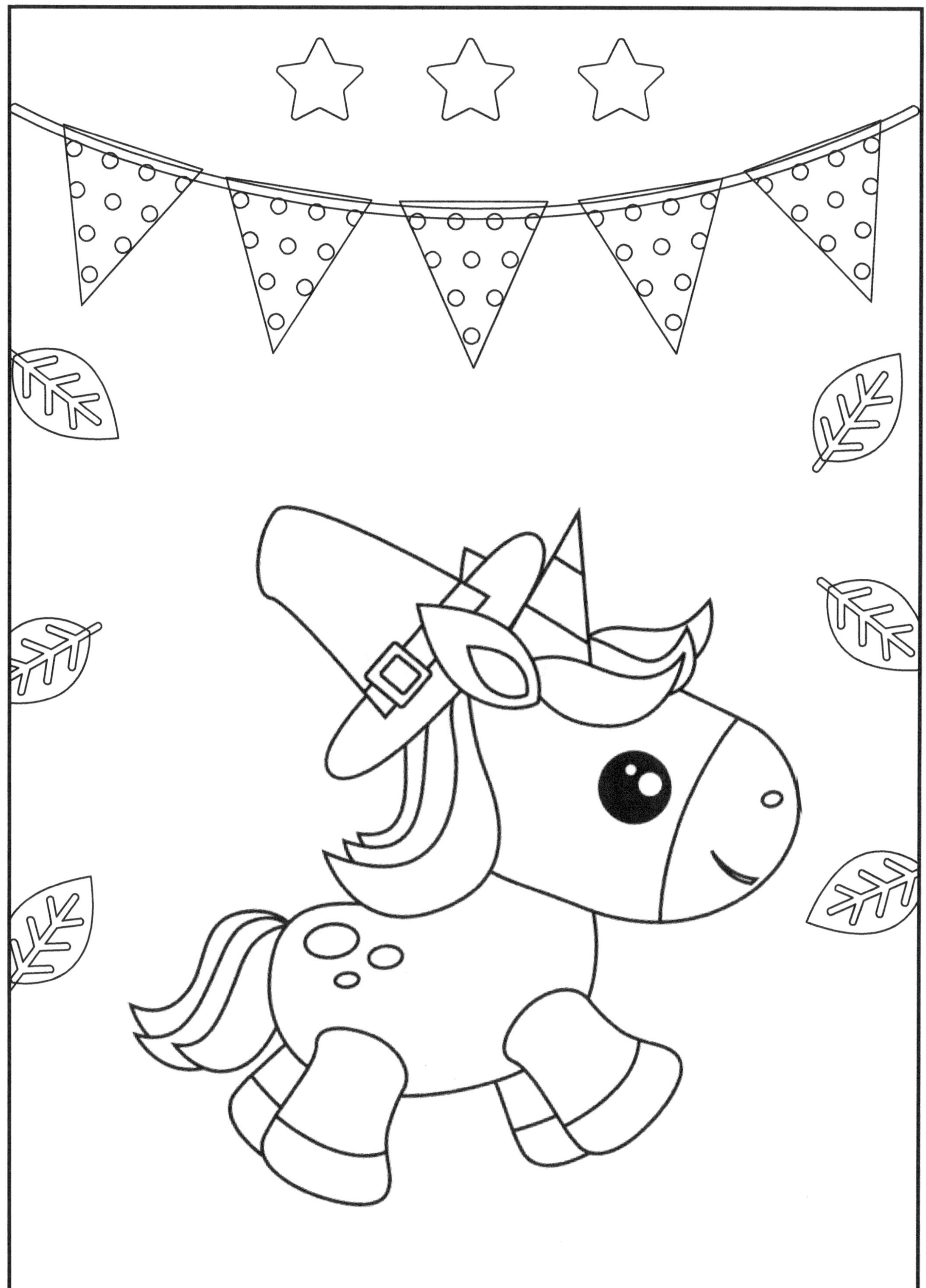

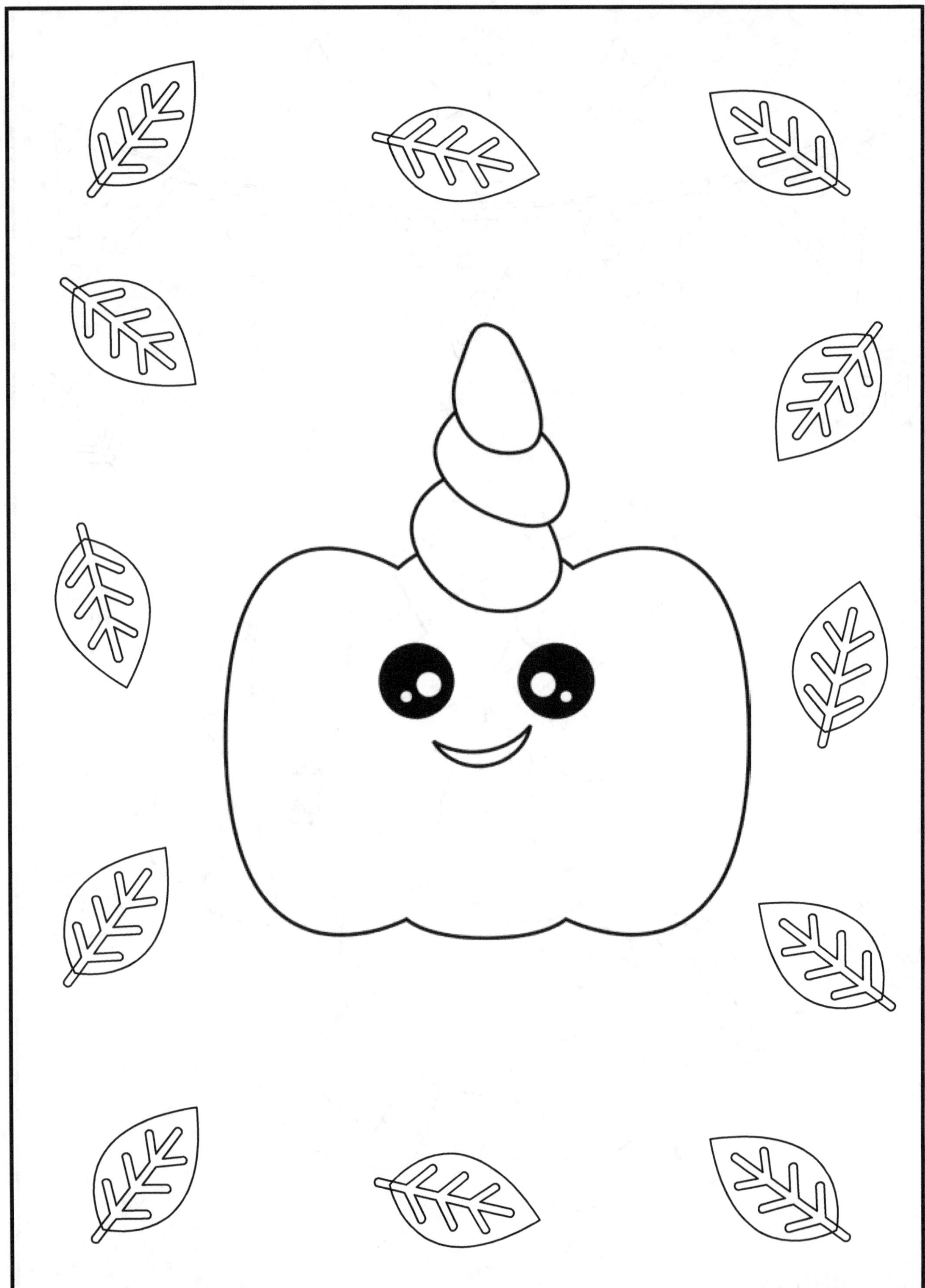

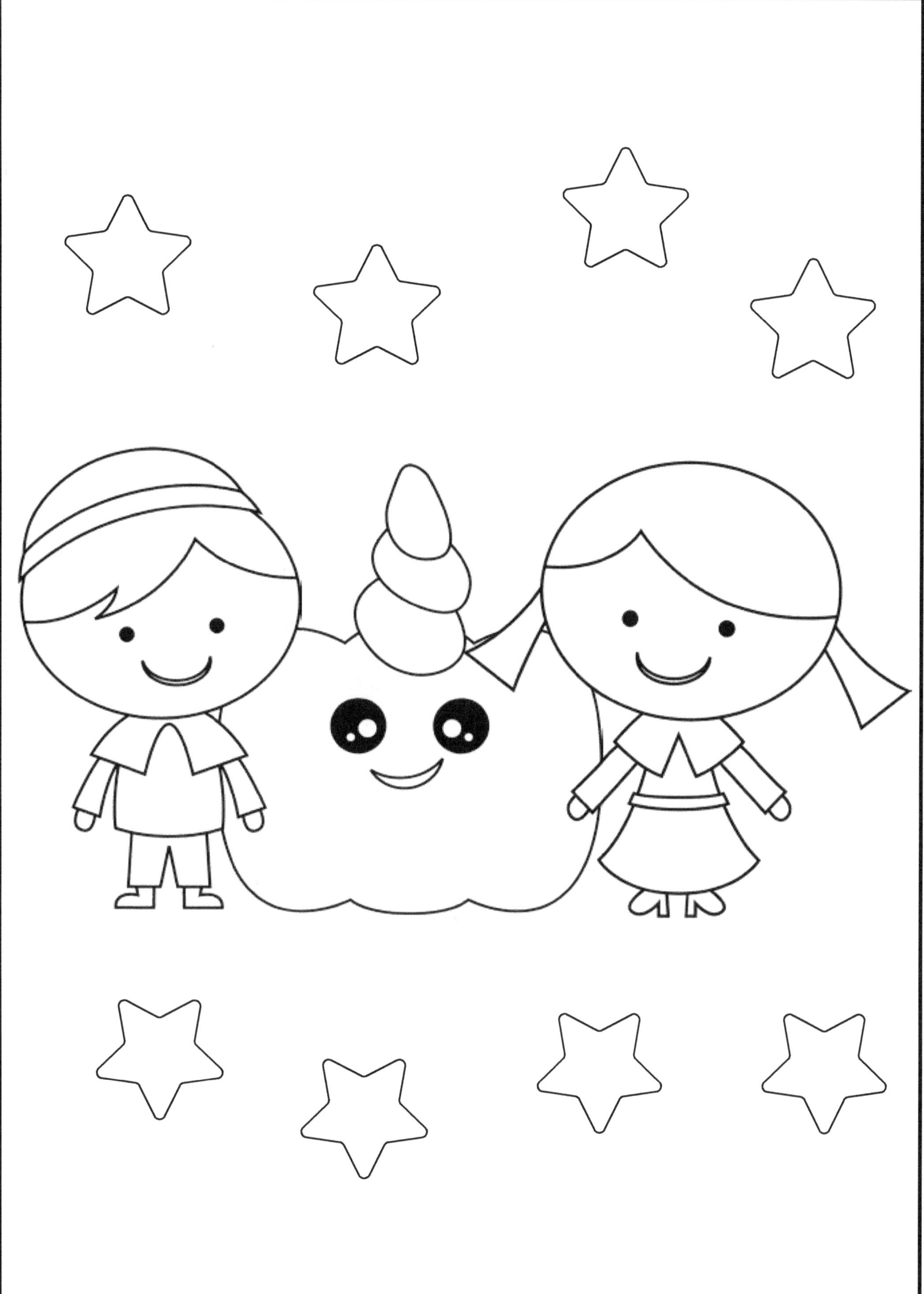

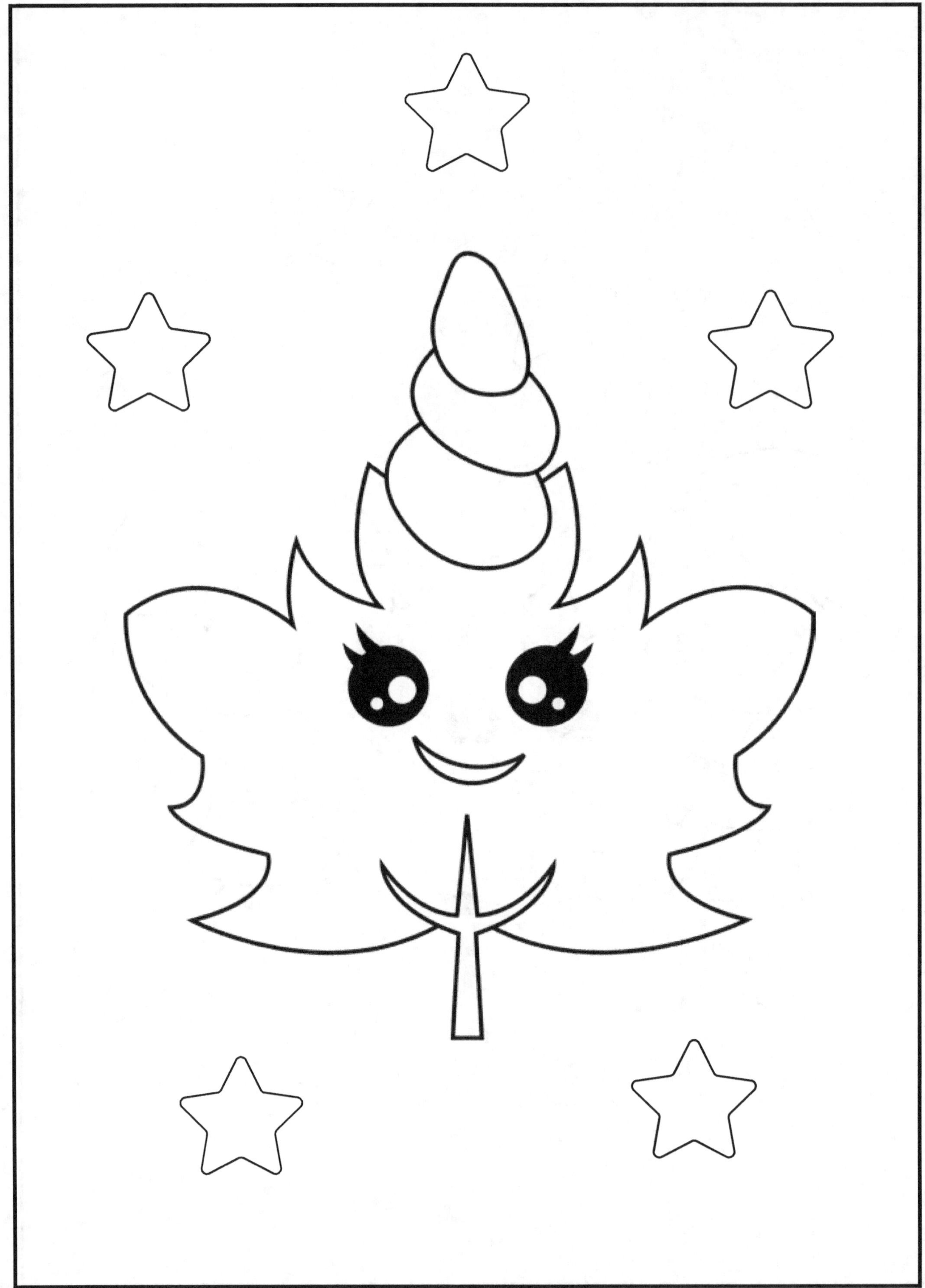

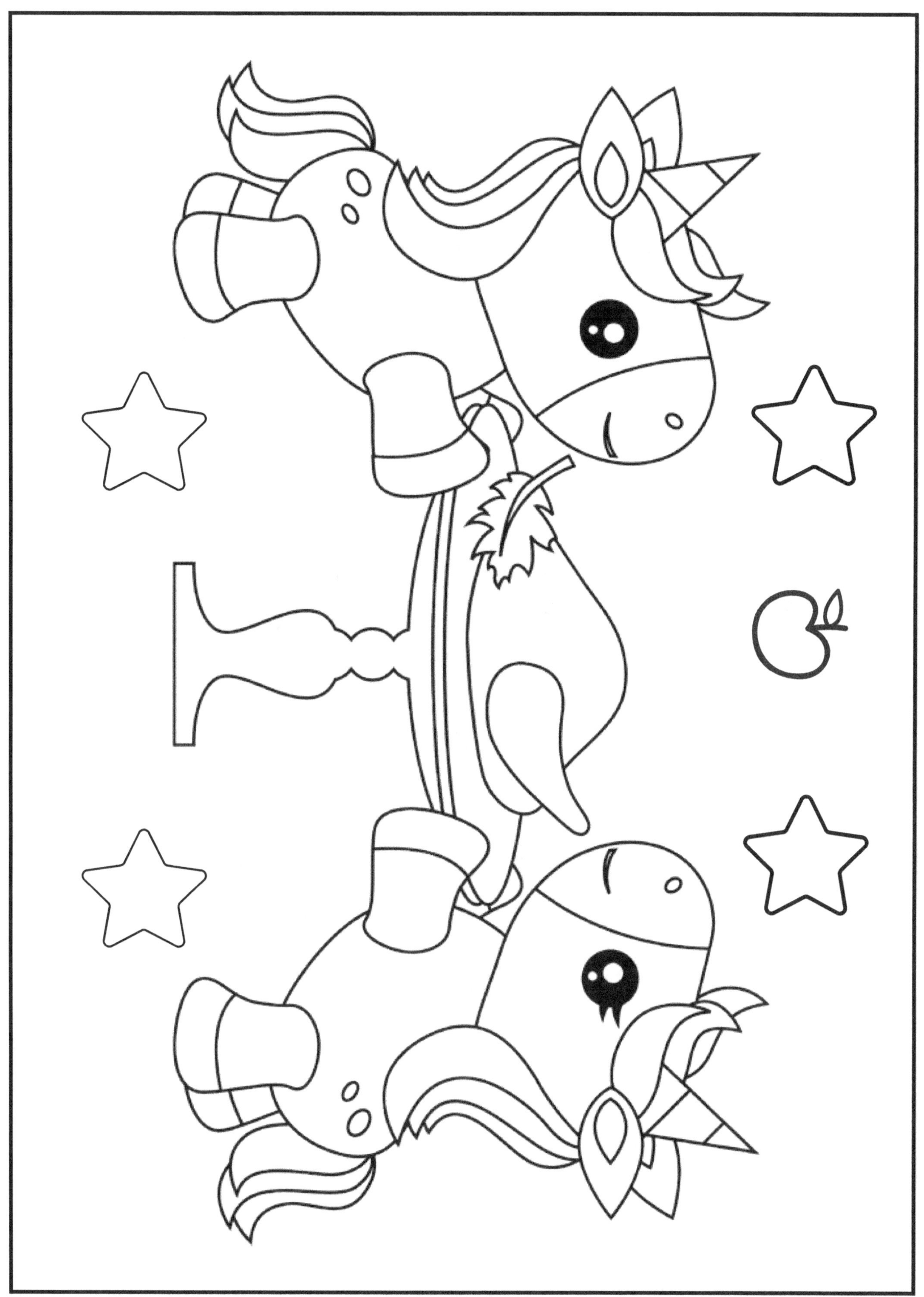

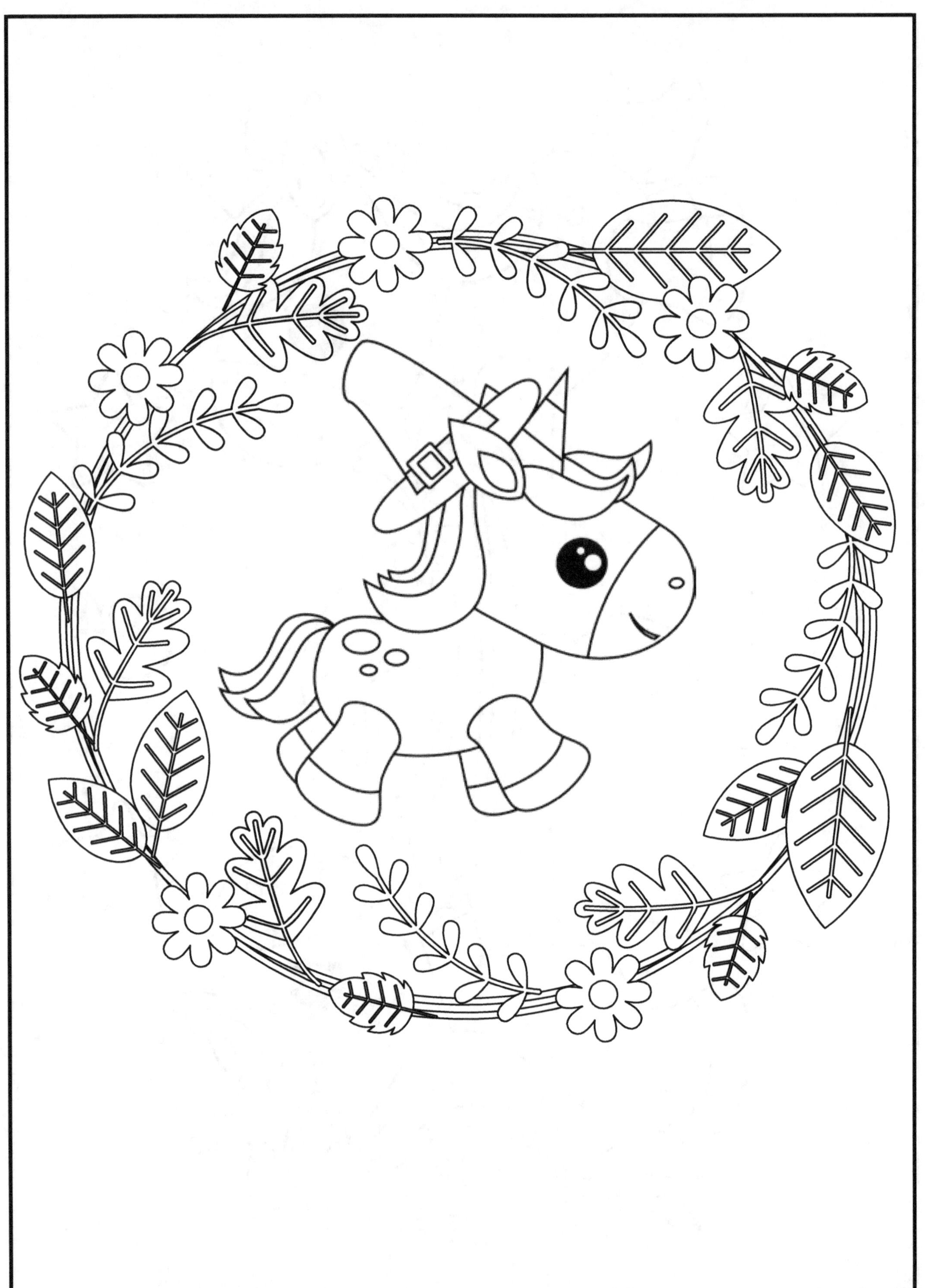

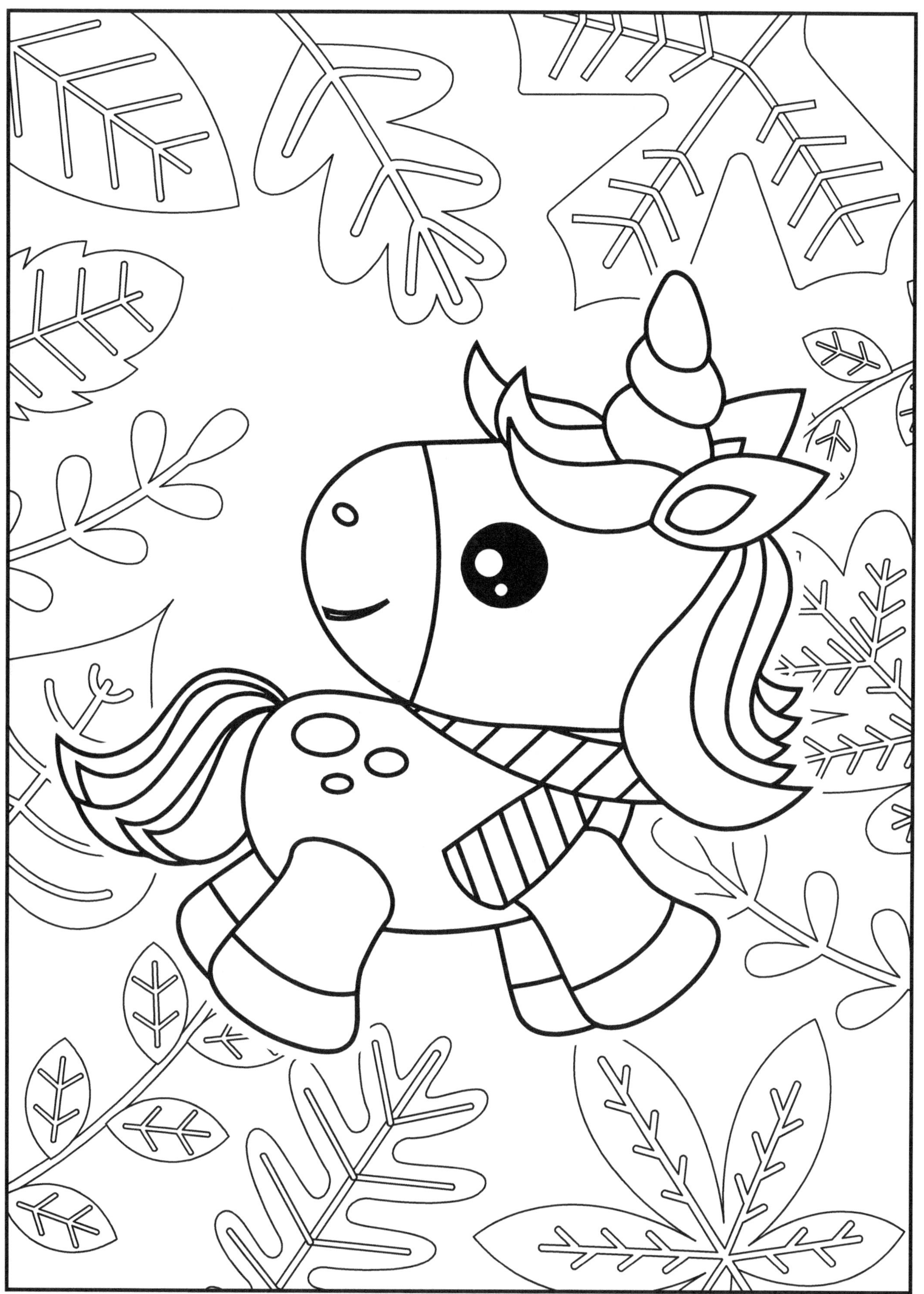

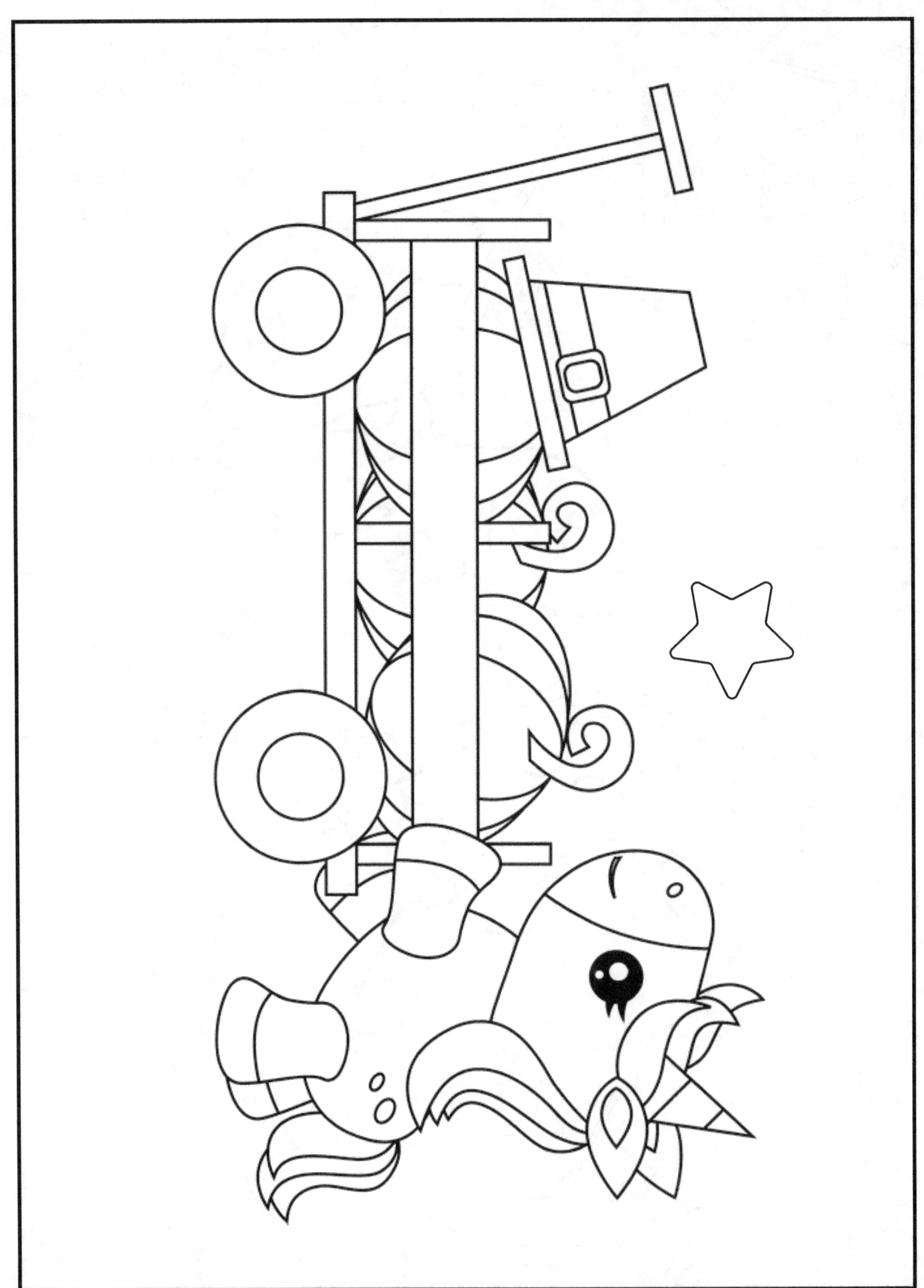

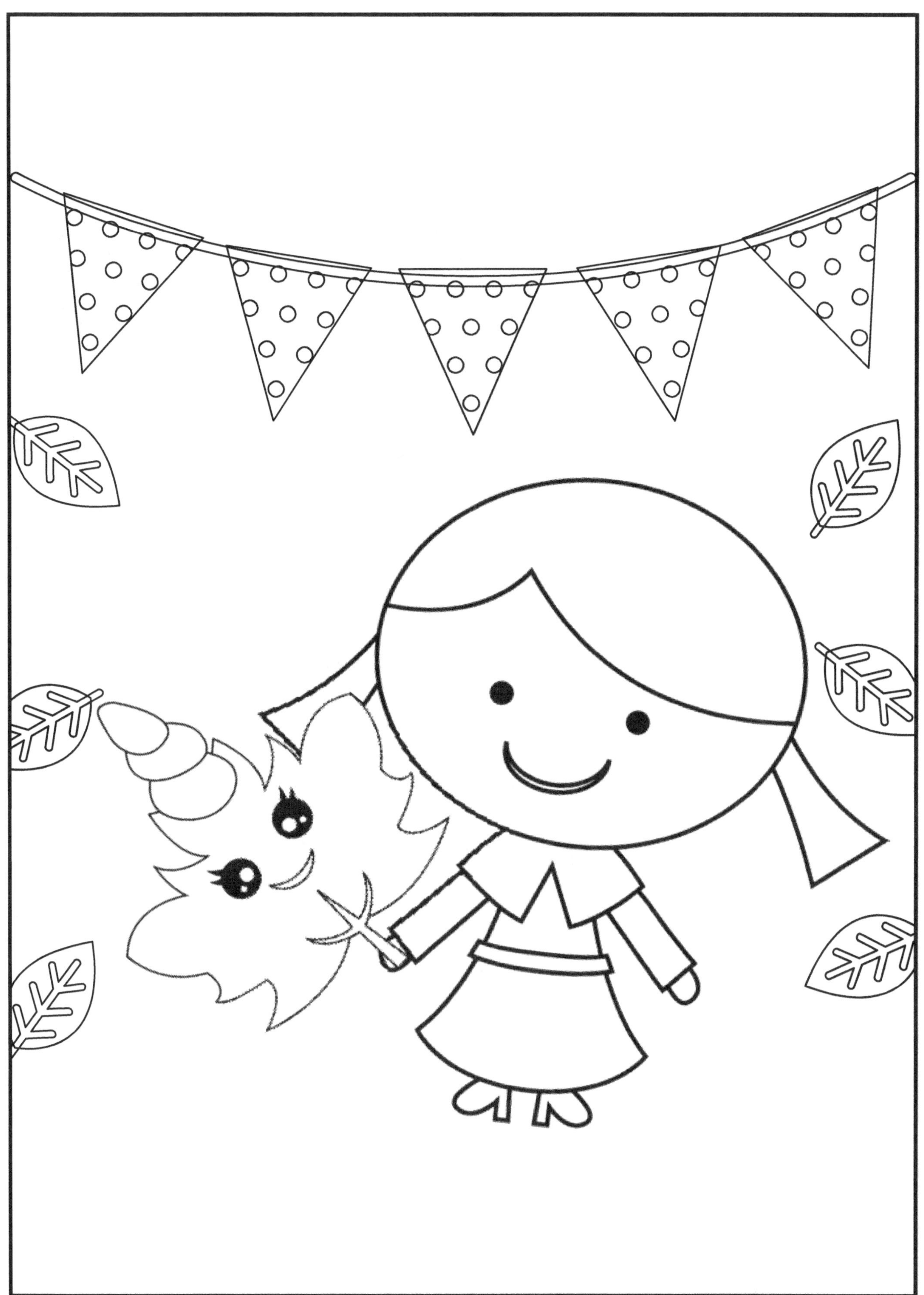

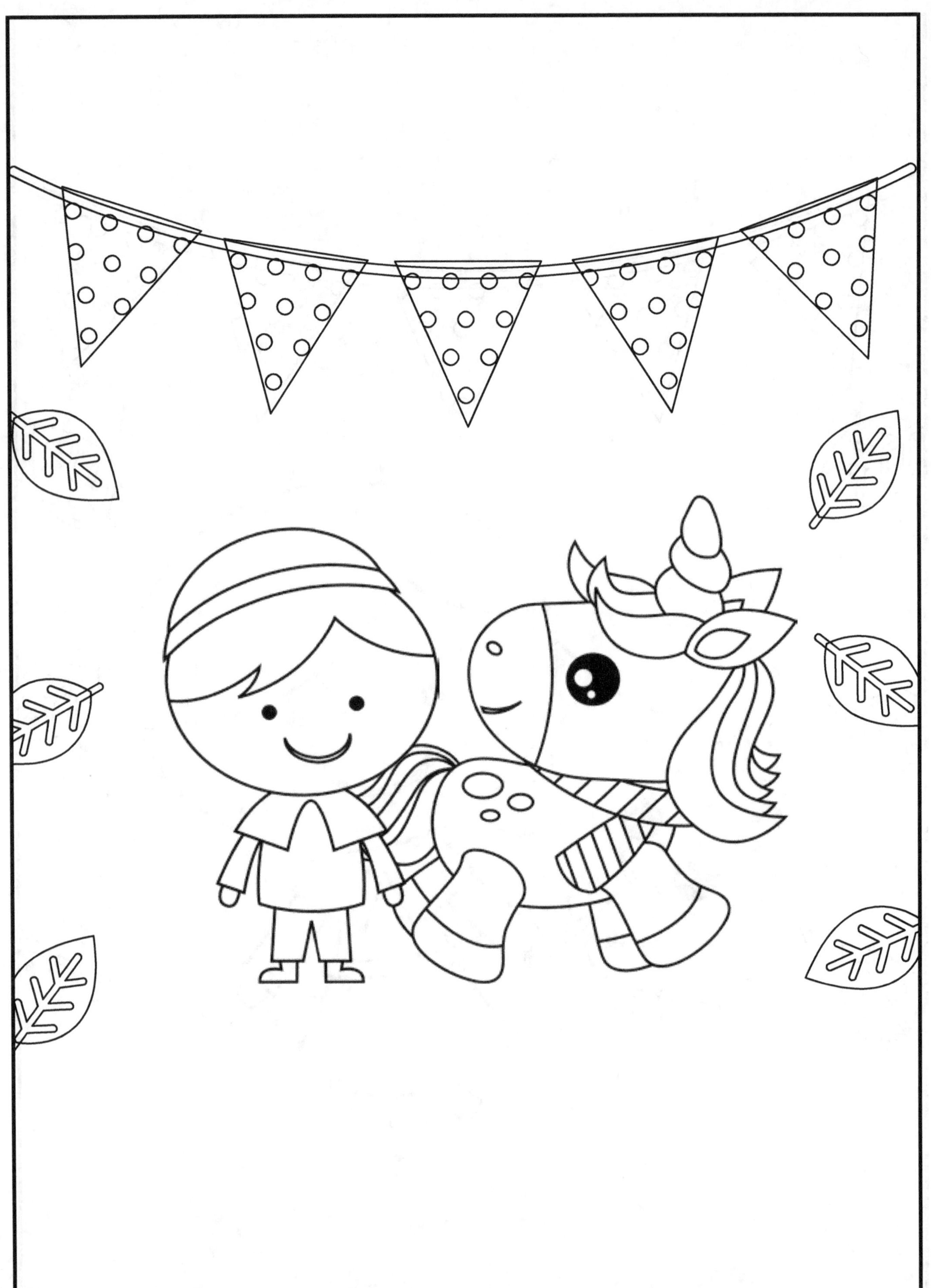

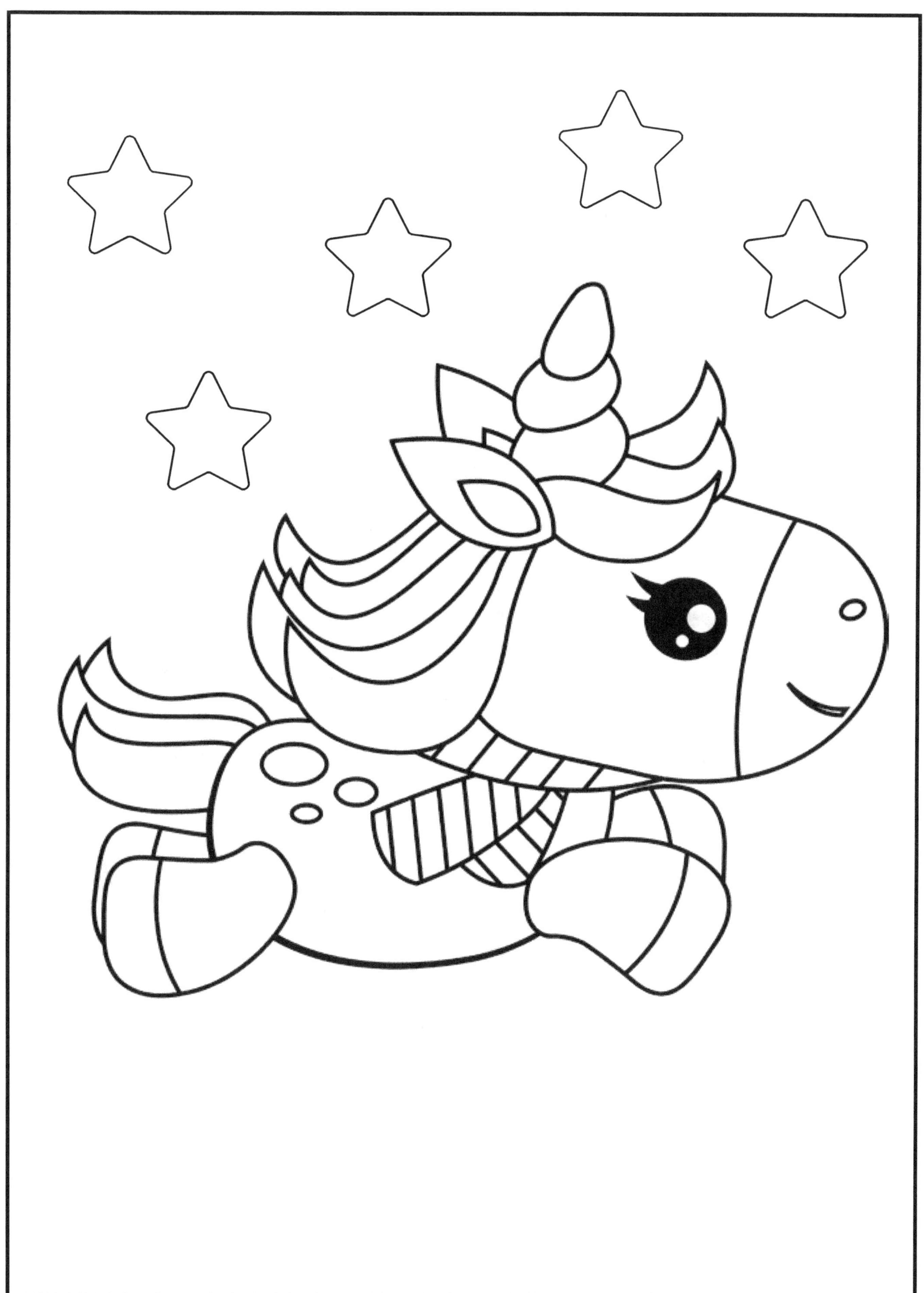

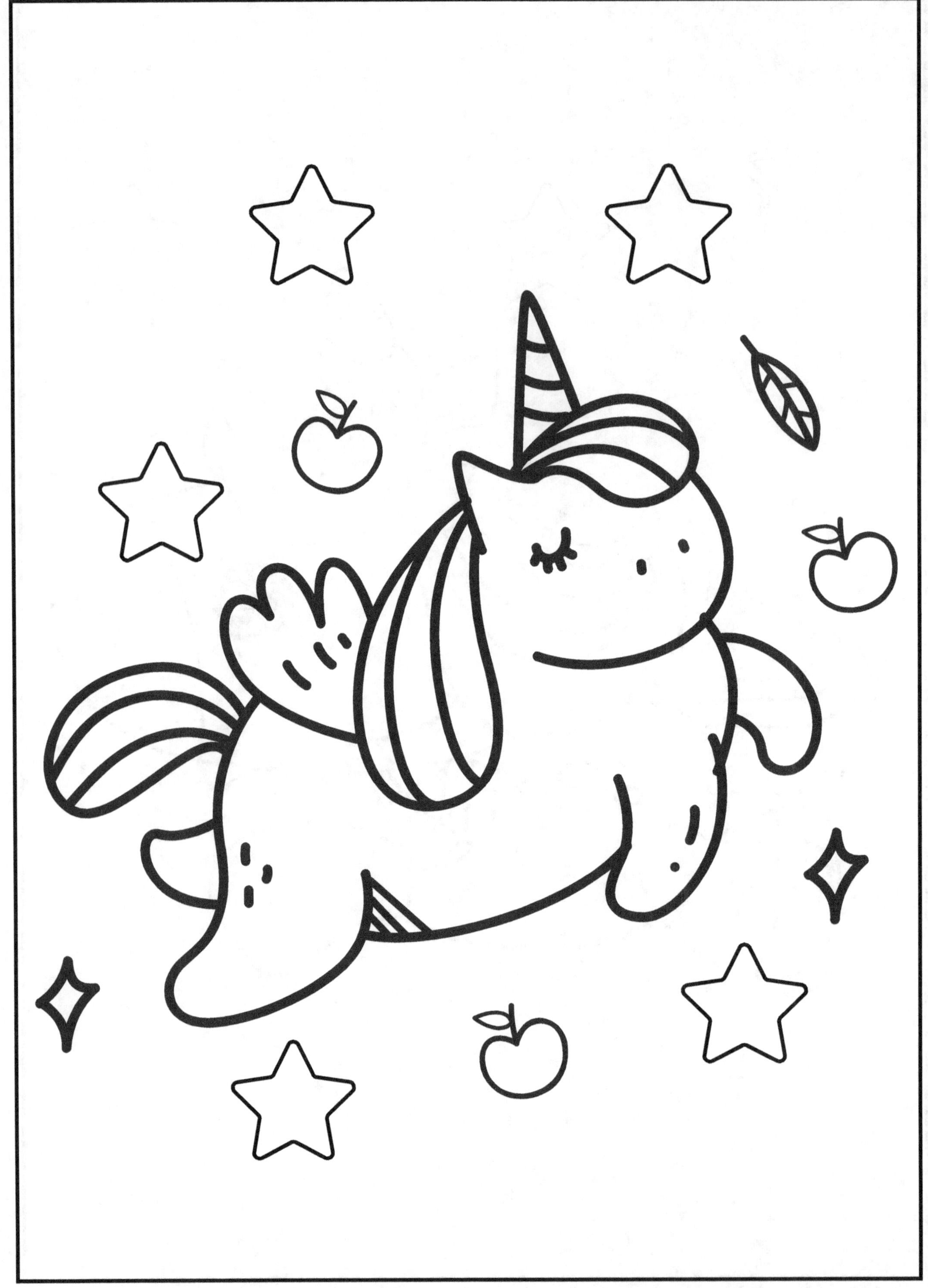

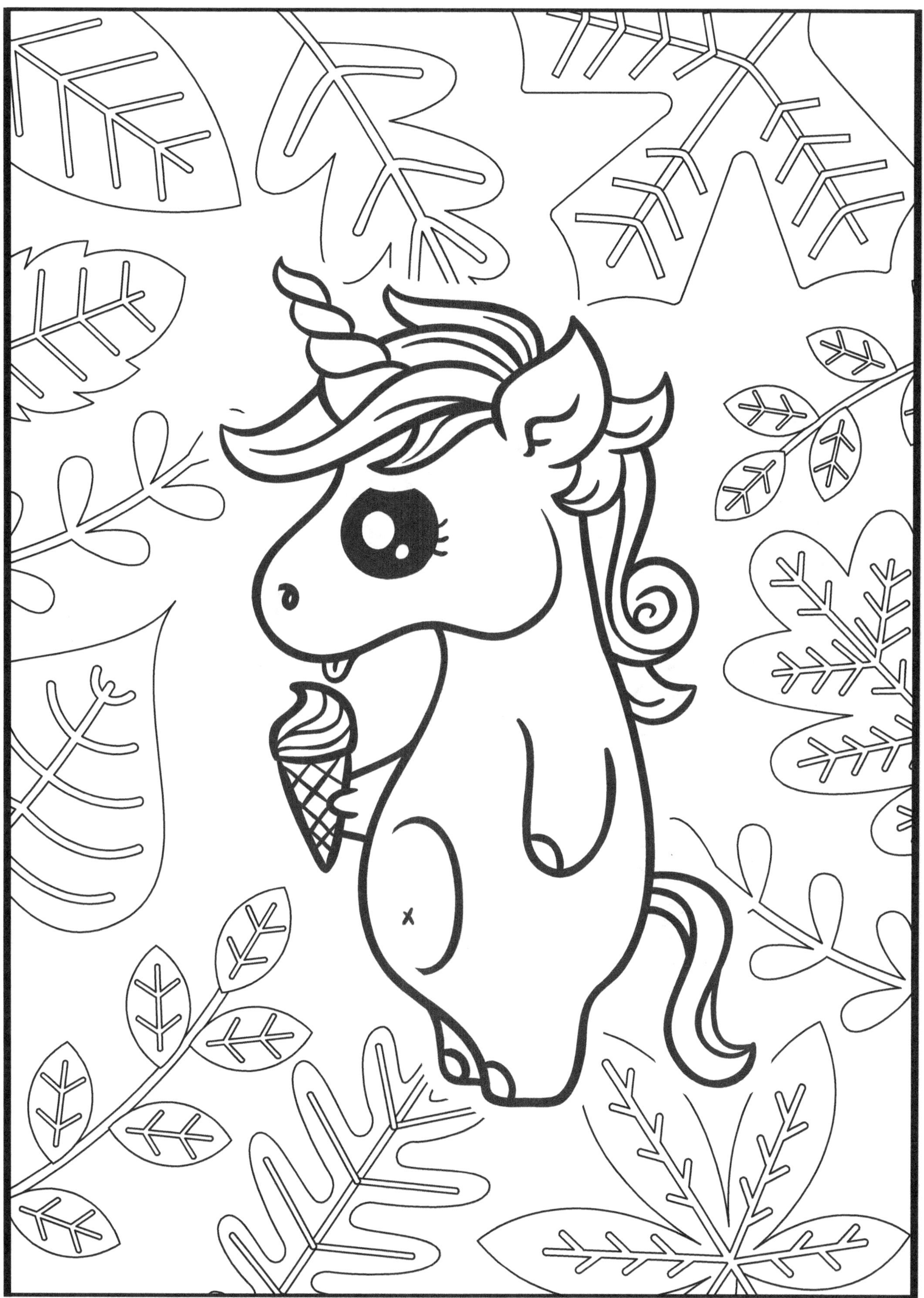

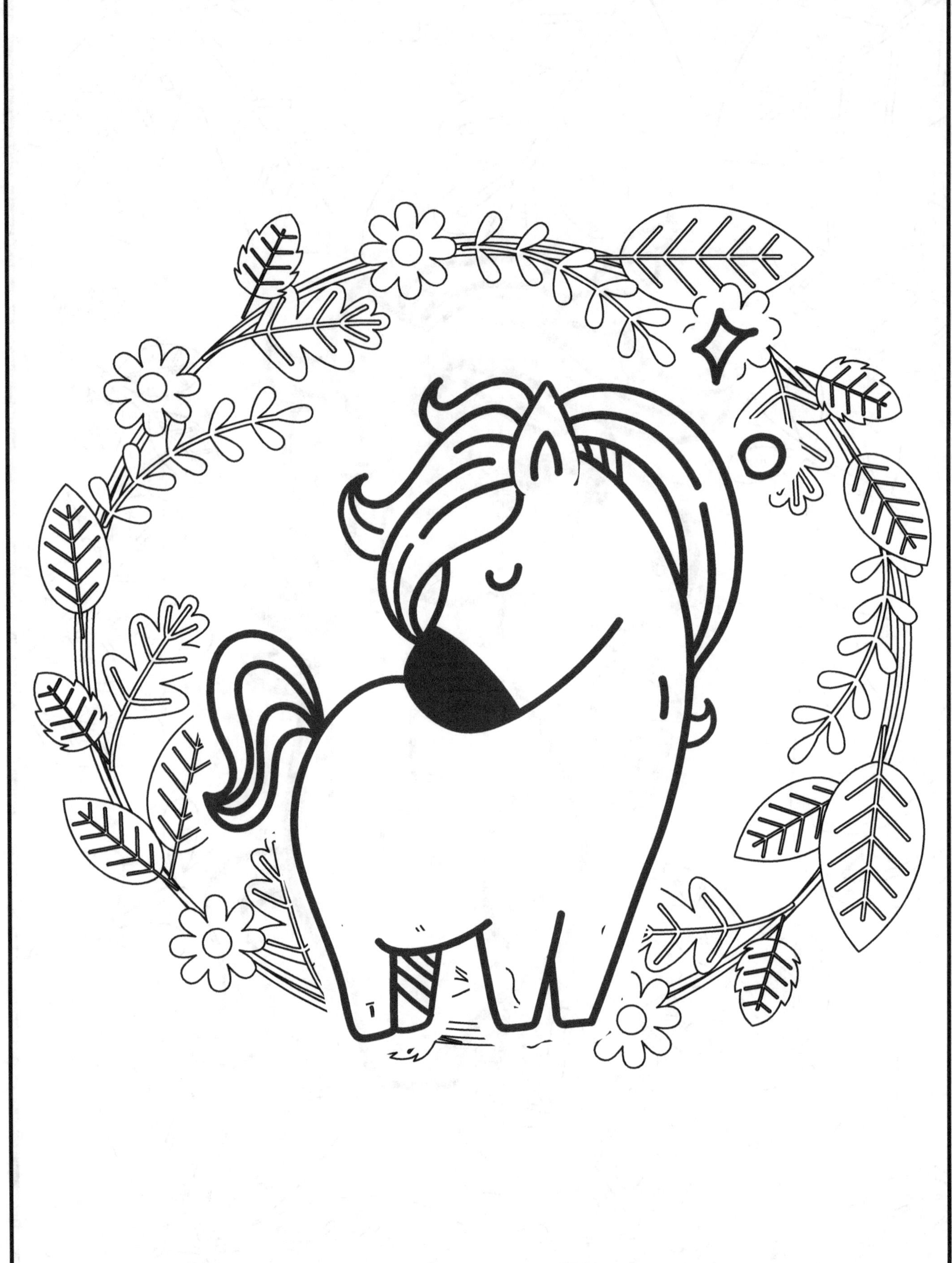

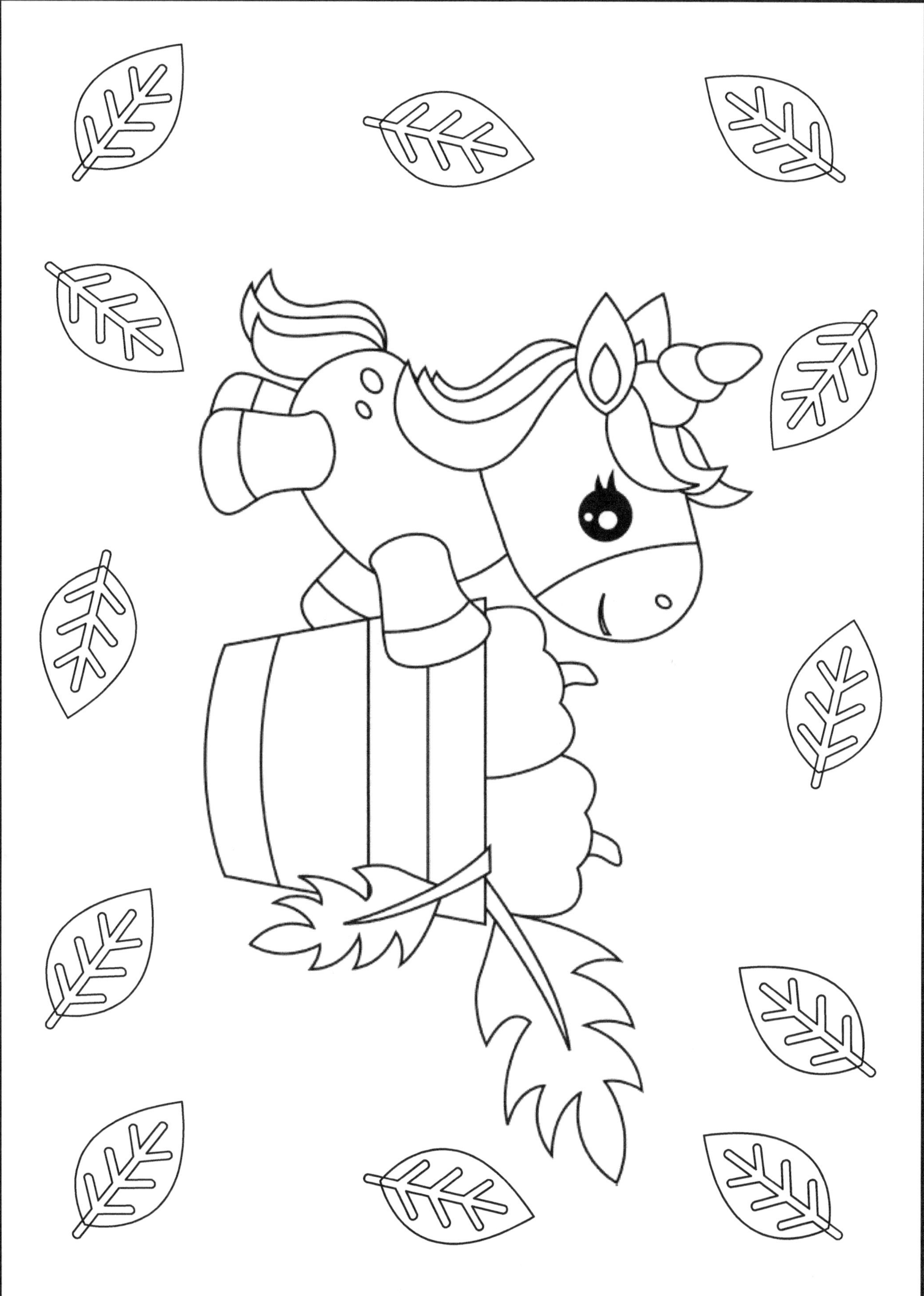

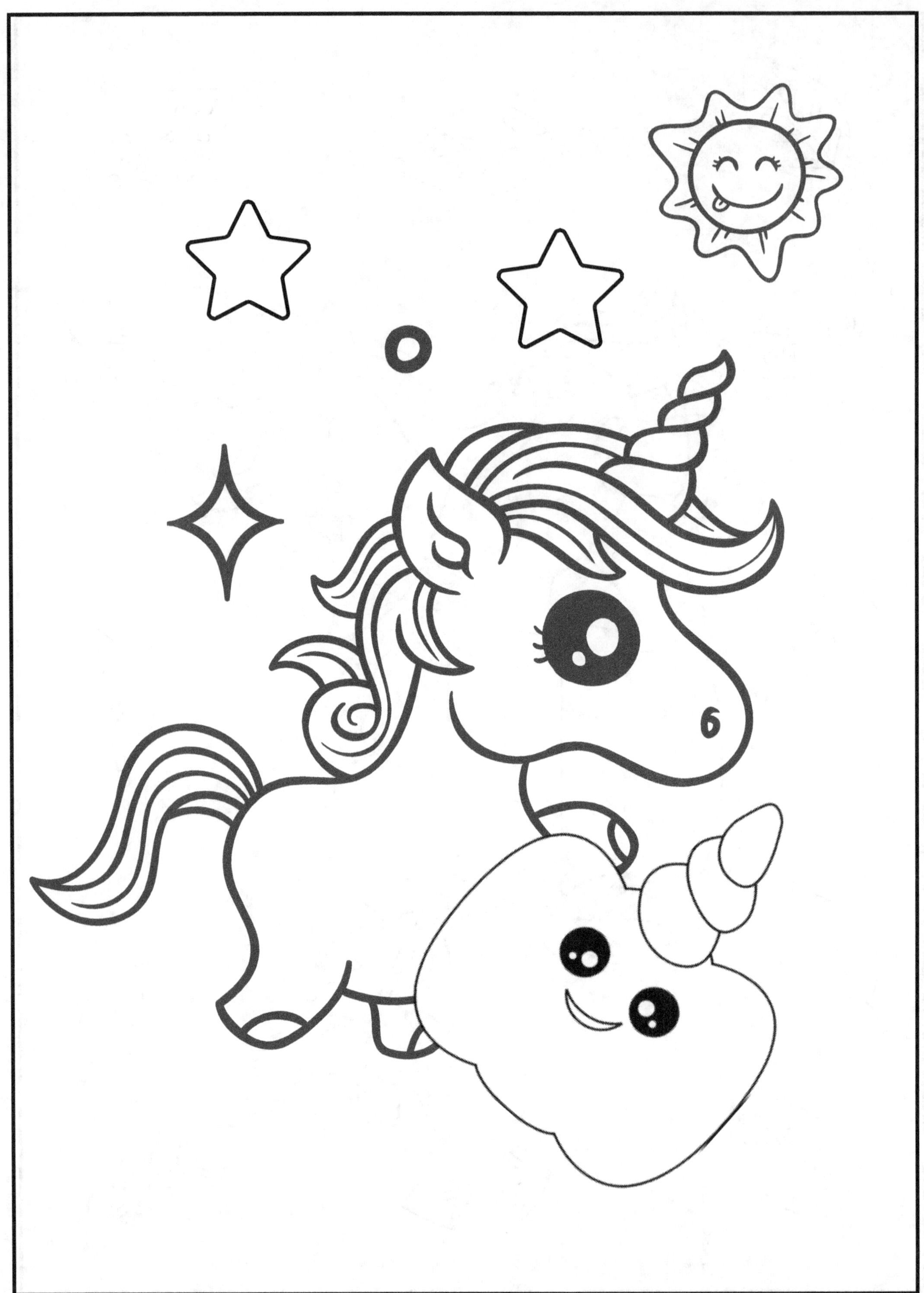

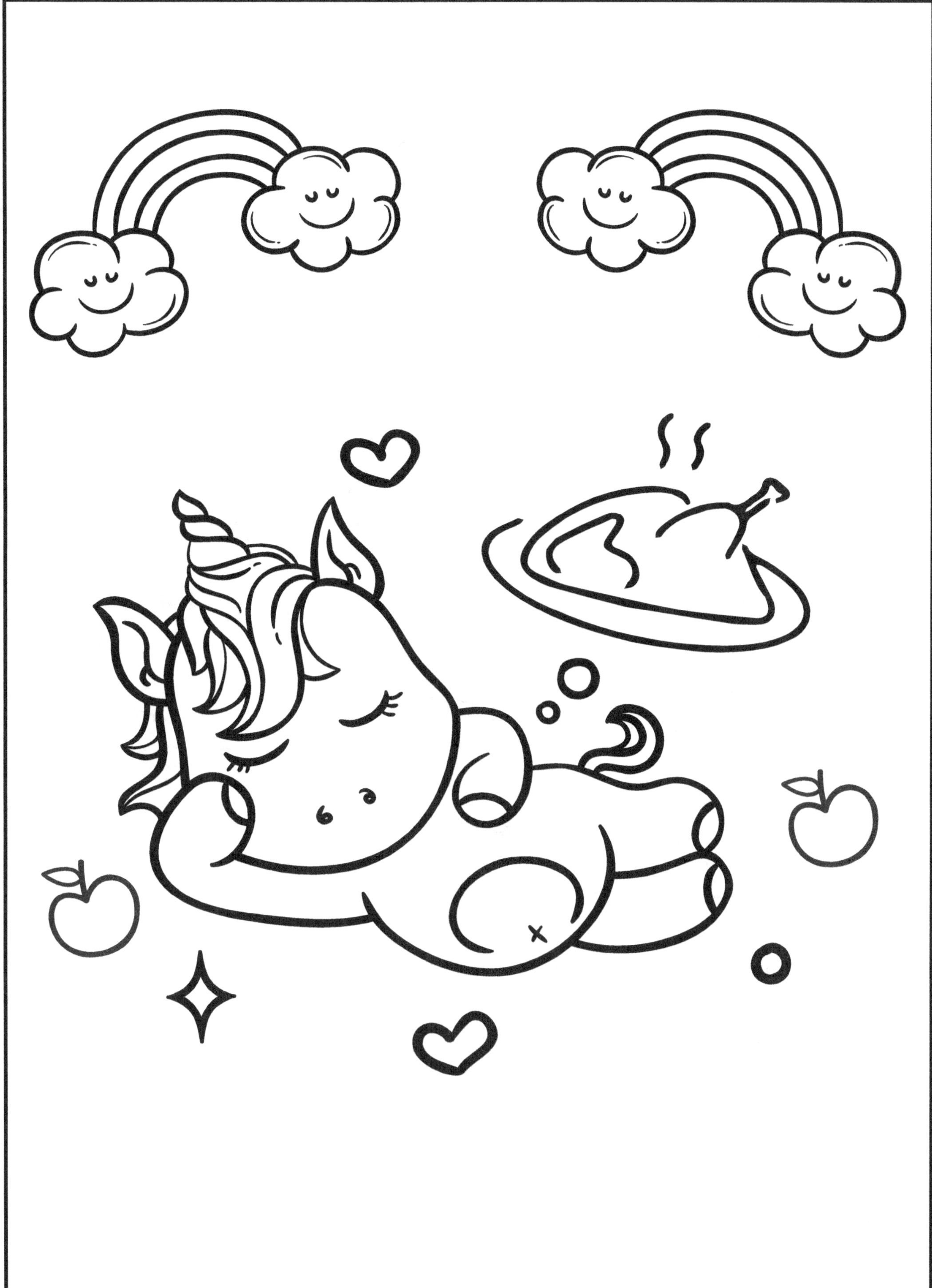

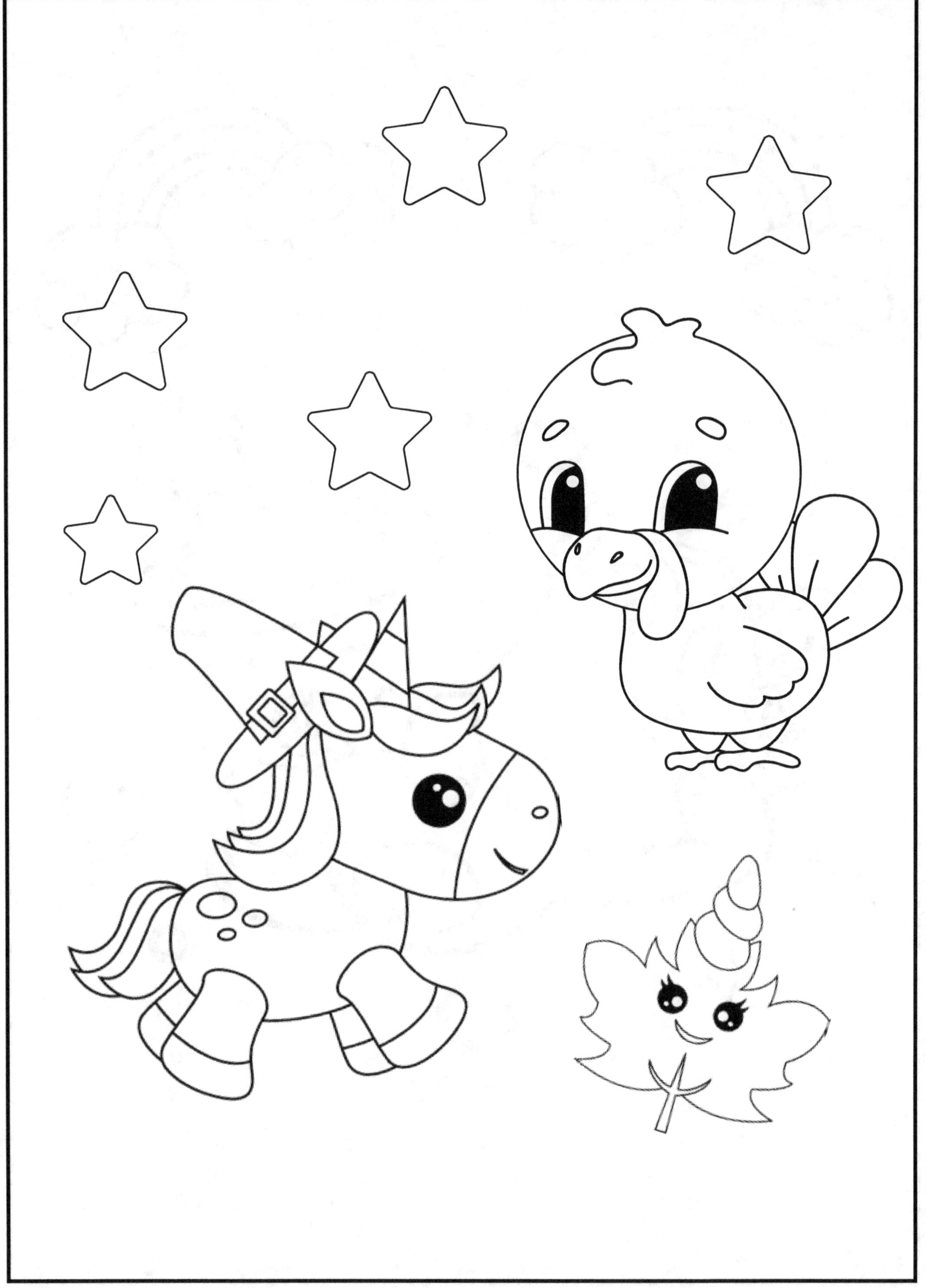

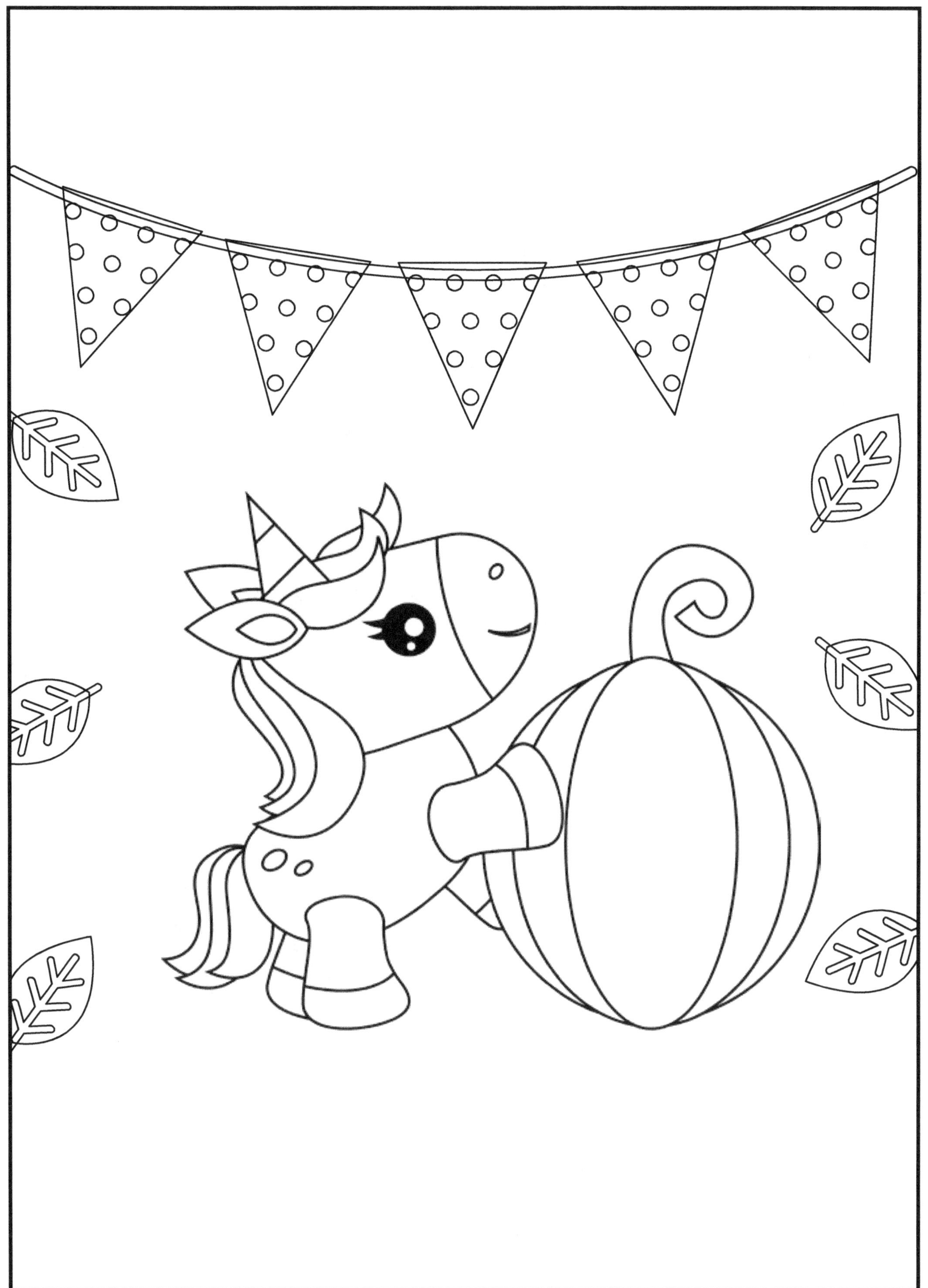

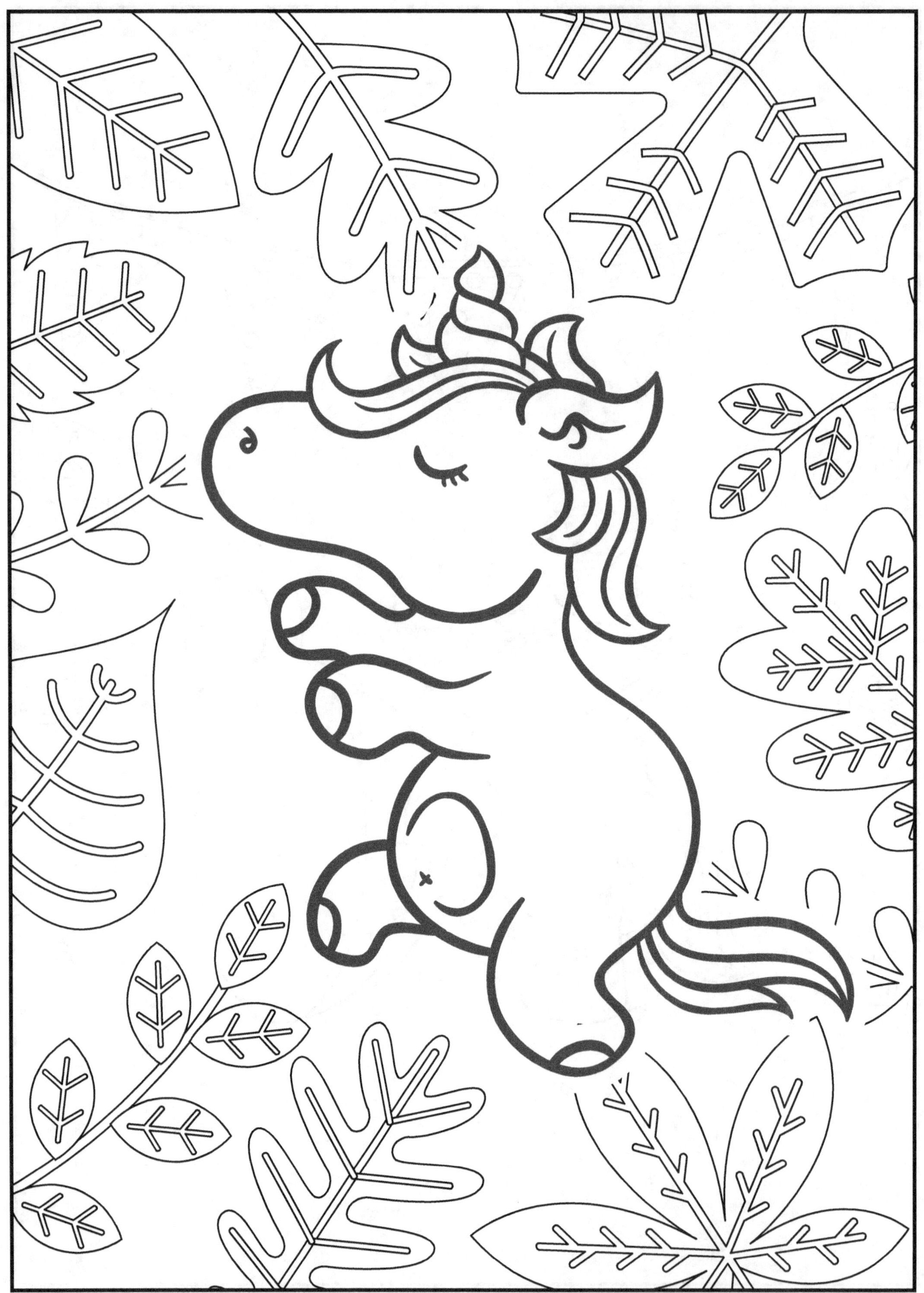

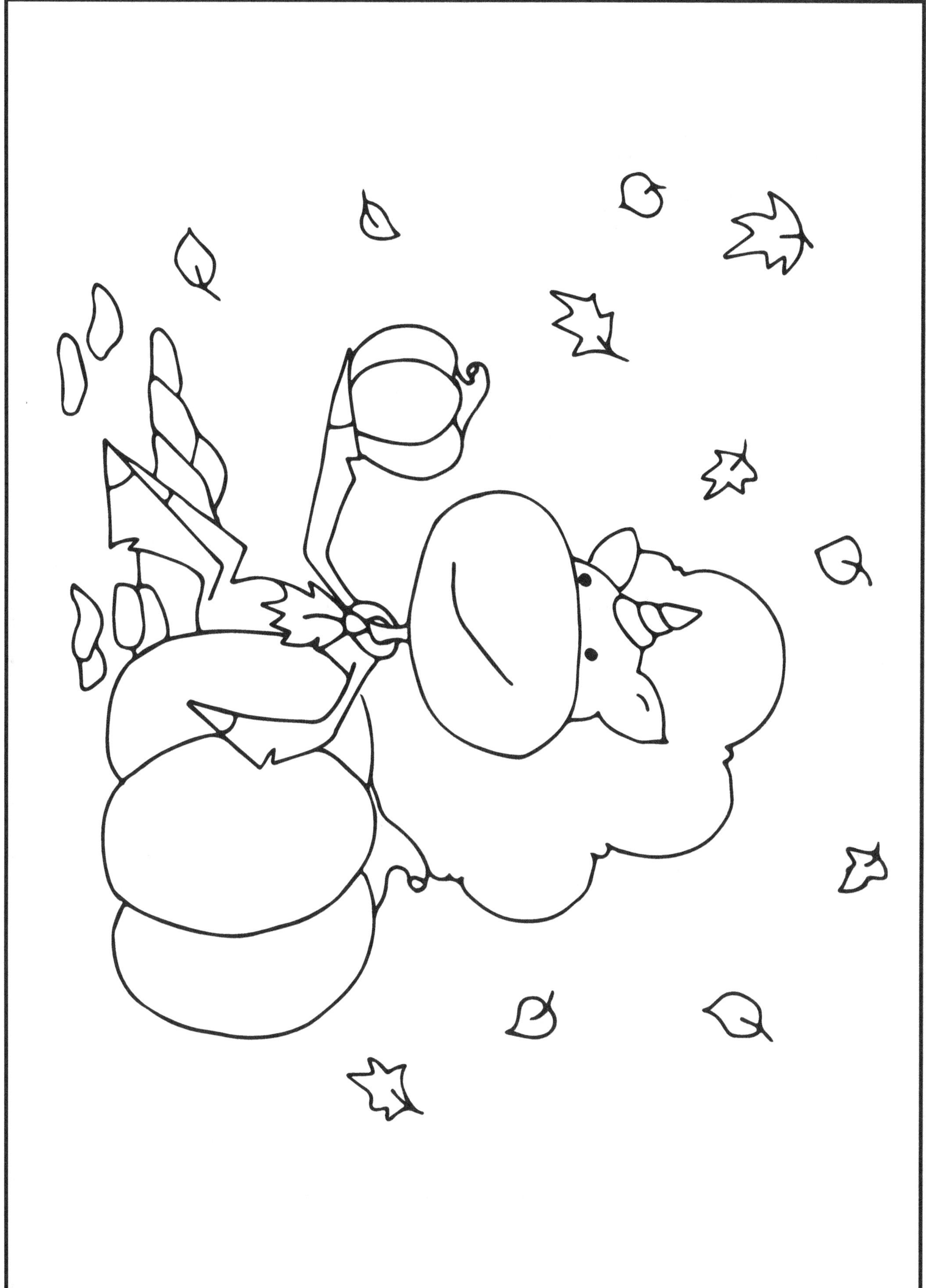

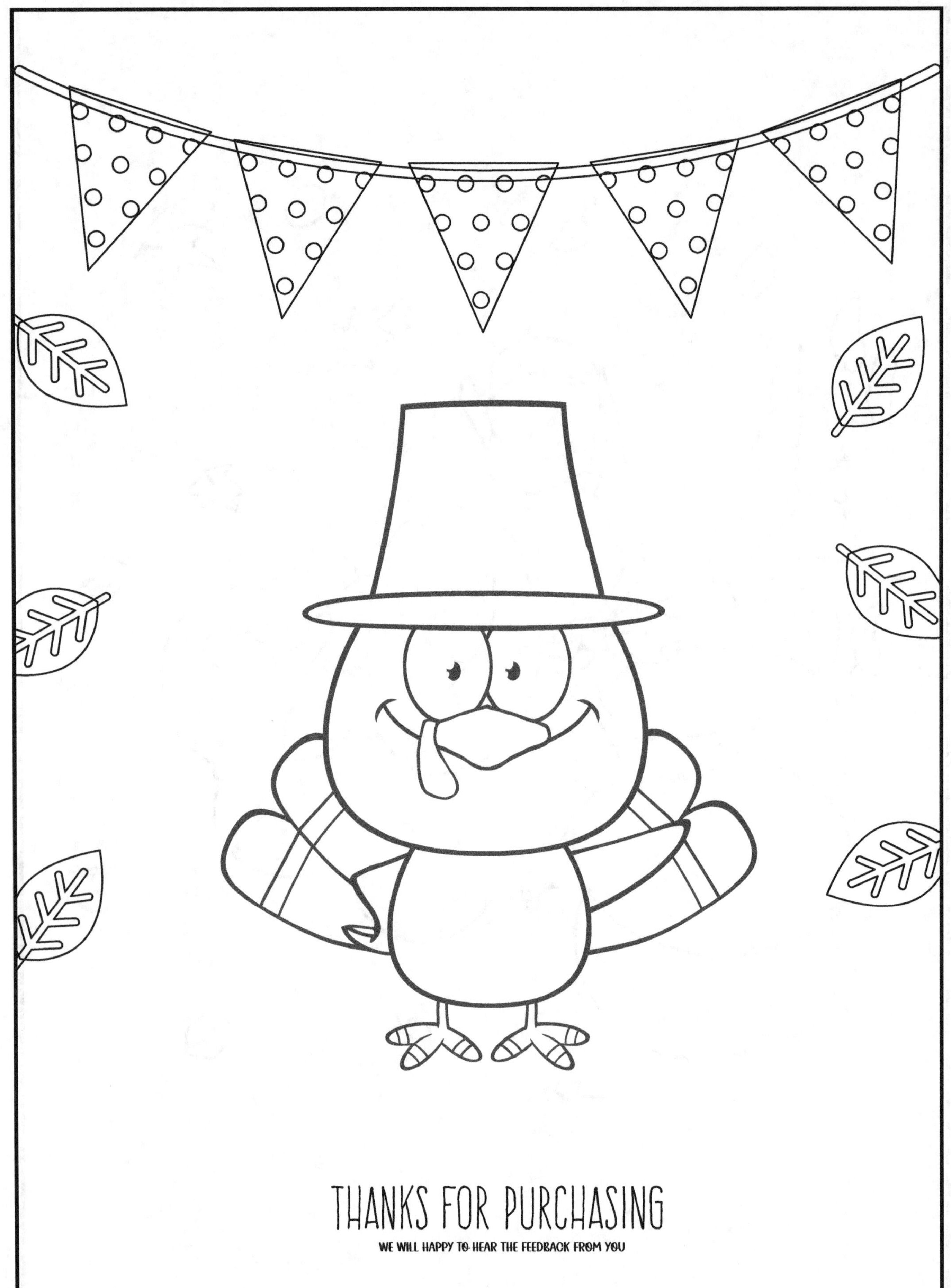

THANKS FOR PURCHASING

WE WILL HAPPY TO HEAR THE FEEDBACK FROM YOU